Anabaptist Meditations

About *Anabaptist Meditations*

Five hundred years ago, a movement emerged in Europe that took seriously the call to follow in the footsteps of Christ. The Anabaptists developed a new form of Christian spirituality and practice in response to the political changes, spiritual confusion, violence, and the economic disparities that they saw around them. Their new faith went beyond carefully crafted creedal statements and instead, they developed a new understanding of Christian discipleship based on their reading of the New Testament and centered on the life and teachings of Christ.

In *Anabaptist Meditations*, Colin Godwin offers thirty devotional readings carefully crafted to guide you to the heart of the Anabaptist tradition. Five themes will challenge you to a more engaged and Christ-centered spiritual life: choosing faith (voluntarism), following Christ (discipleship), Christian community (church), separation (nonresistance), and witness (mission).

Each entry begins with a biblical passage, followed by a short meditation and quotation from an Anabaptist writer, and concludes with questions for reflection and a prayer. *Anabaptist Meditations* provides a devotional complement to the Anabaptist tradition that draws on its past to inform our present.

"Colin Godwin's *Anabaptist Meditations* provides an accessible and attractive set of devotional readings that integrate biblical, historical, and contemporary reflections alongside discussion questions designed to provoke deeper engagement. The book is a very helpful introduction to Anabaptist spirituality."

—Stuart Murray, author of *Biblical Interpretation in the Anabaptist Tradition* (Pandora Press, 2000) and *The Naked Anabaptist* (Herald Press, 2010).

Anabaptist Meditations

Thirty days of Biblical Reflection
from the Founders of the Tradition

Colin Godwin

PANDORA PRESS

Author: Colin Godwin

Book design, cover, and editing by Maxwell Kennel

The author and publisher gratefully acknowledge the financial support for this title provided by
Carey Theological College.

ANABAPTIST MEDITATIONS
ISBN: 978-1-77873-001-6

Copyright © 2022 Pandora Press
Published by Pandora Press
All rights reserved.
www.pandorapress.com

Table of Contents

Introduction

Part I. Choosing Faith (Voluntarism)
1. Freedom to Believe
2. Freedom to Disagree
3. The Holy Spirit and Human Initiative
4. Struggling with sin
5. Choosing Baptism
6. Faith for the Common Person

Part II. Following Christ (Discipleship)
7. The Primacy of Scripture
8. Christ's Return and Discipleship
9. Radical Obedience
10. Standing Firm
11. Keeping your Word when it Hurts
12. Faith under Pressure

Part III. Christian Community (Church)
13. Saying 'Our Father' means Sharing
14. New Monasticism
15. Church Discipline
16. Restoration
17. Unbelieving Children
18. Generosity

Part IV. Separation (Nonresistance)
19. Rejecting violence
20. Separation of Church and State
21. Spiritual Weapons
22. Christians in Government
23. Disagreeing Peacefully
24. God's justice, not ours

Part V. Witness (Mission)
25. Saving and Serving
26. Witness in Word and Deed
27. Give us this Day your Holy Word
28. Transforming Witness
29. Welcoming the Broken
30. Jesus is coming: Repent and Believe

Postscript

Bibliography

About the Author

Introduction

In the sixteenth century, Anabaptism emerged as a new and rapidly growing stream of Christianity. Anabaptists sought the renewal and restoration of the church according to a pattern they saw in the New Testament. They promoted high standards for Christian living along with a renewed optimism about the ability of people to follow Christ, especially as expressed through his teachings in the Sermon on the Mount (Matthew 5-7). They did not accept infant baptism. Instead, they insisted that the New Testament defined baptism as a voluntary decision to follow Christ – something that was impossible for infants. Anabaptists rejected violence and vigorously championed a church that was not allied with government or state. This set of convictions put them at odds with other Christians of the time and led to the widespread persecution of Anabaptists by both Catholic and Protestant groups.

Today, the best-known Anabaptists are perhaps the Amish, Mennonites, and Hutterites. Since the middle of the twentieth century, scholars, church leaders, and lay people have shown a renewed interest in Anabaptist writings on topics such as Christian discipleship, pacifism (or nonresistance), the sharing of goods, mission, and the separation of church and state. Many people have been influenced by Anabaptist convictions, both inside and outside formal groups who identify with the tradition.

My own interest in Anabaptist history and theology deepened during my Ph.D. studies at the International Baptist Theological Seminary in Prague, which I concluded while serving as a Canadian Baptist missionary in Rwanda. My thesis was published as *Baptizing, Gathering and Sending: the significance of Anabaptist approaches to mission in the sixteenth-century context* (Kitchener, ON: Pandora Press, 2012). Alongside my academic research, I found myself personally challenged by a number of Anabaptist writers. To capture my reflections on the value of Anabaptist spirituality, I took devotional notes in the margins of my research.

Those devotional thoughts have resulted in this book. It includes thirty Anabaptist meditations, divided into five key themes: choosing faith (voluntarism), following Christ (discipleship), Christian community (church), separation (nonresistance), and witness (mission). Each entry begins with a biblical passage, followed by a short meditation and quotation from an Anabaptist writer. In a few instances, where the Anabaptist author did not make a clear reference to a particular biblical text, I chose a biblical text that other

Anabaptists commonly connected with the same theme. I close each entry with some questions for personal or group reflection, and a prayer.

The historical and theological background provided for each entry is necessarily brief. If you wish to learn more, I recommend Arnold Snyder's *Anabaptist History and Theology: An Introduction* (Kitchener, ON: Pandora Press, 1995). For a contemporary exploration of Anabaptism geared to both those inside and outside the tradition, I encourage you to read Stuart Murray's *The Naked Anabaptist* (Scottdale, Pa: Herald Press, 2010).

Each Anabaptist writer mentioned in this book had a complicated life and sometimes struggled to be faithful to the gospel message. I do not mean to present these early Anabaptists as saints. They made mistakes and were not always consistent. They were products of their time in ways that challenge the ideas of our time, and in ways that deserve to be critiqued. Nevertheless, they were passionate about living out the gospel as they understood it, even when it was difficult to do so. I was challenged by that passion and devotion, and I hope you will be too.

Five hundred years ago, these early Anabaptists sought to be faithful to Christ. Today, I believe that their voices can still challenge us to do the same. In the words of Menno Simons, I encourage you to…

Take the Lord Jesus Christ as an example and follow His footsteps; walk as He walked, for to this end did Moses and all the prophets preach, to this end did the Son of God come down from heaven and the holy apostles were sent forth. To this end was baptism and the Lord's Supper instituted by the mouth of the Lord, so that we, admonished by it, might awake, repent and lead an unblameable, pious life in all righteousness. Be ye holy; for I am holy says the Lord.[1]

Menno Simons
Encouragement to Christian Believers (1556)

---

[1] Menno Simons, "Encouragement to Christian Believers (1556)," in *The Complete Writings of Menno Simons, C. 1496-1561*, ed. J. C. Wenger and Harold Stauffer Bender (Scottdale, Pa.; Kitchener, ON: Herald Press, 1986), 1045.

Part I
Choosing Faith
(Voluntarism)

While it may not seem to be an unusual belief today, the Anabaptist conviction that each person had a personal responsibility to choose to be a Christian was a radical concept in the religious, political, and social world of the sixteenth century. Anabaptist preachers did not rely on governments to impose or support their beliefs. They did not accept that citizens in each territory were automatically followers of the same faith as their ruler. Instead, Anabaptists called people to a conscious decision of faith, conversion, baptism, and participation in a local church.

In many cases, the personal decision to follow Christ resulted in persecution by civil authorities or by other Christians. All of the Anabaptist authors represented in this first section were persecuted. Menno Simons died a natural death but lived most of his life as a fugitive. Balthasar Hubmaier was burned at the stake, Hans Schlaffer was beheaded, and Peter Glock was jailed for nineteen years.

Instead of relying upon rulers to impose their faith, Anabaptist preachers baptized consenting converts and gathered believers into new church communities. For Anabaptists, personal decision was essential for true Christian discipleship. A true church could not exist without it. In the words of Hans Schlaffer,

> O Almighty, eternal God, we acknowledge our weakness and ask you to strengthen us with your Holy Spirit to deliver us from human fear. O eternal God, forgive us from all our sin. O Almighty Father, we pray also for our enemies. Forgive them, for they do not know what they are doing. We pray also for all people of good heart, for they hunger and thirst for your divine righteousness. Satisfy them with that food of eternal life which never spoils. O eternal, heavenly Father, we give you praise, honor and thanks that you have graciously called us out of the terrible darkness of this world into your wonderful light, which you have kept hidden from the wise of this world but have revealed to the common person.[2]

Hans Schlaffer,
Two Prayers (1527)

---

[2] Hans Schlaffer, "Two Prayers (1527)," in *Early Anabaptist Spirituality: Selected Writings*, ed. Daniel Liechty (New York: Paulist Press, 1994), 109.

Day 1
Freedom to Believe
(Balthasar Hubmaier)

The thief comes only to steal and kill and destroy; I have come that they may have life, and have it to the full. —John 10:10

Swiss Anabaptist Balthasar Hubmaier wrote in defense of religious freedom, while arguing that Christians who used violence to make converts were disobeying the teachings of Christ. In Hubmaier's *On Heretics and Those Who Burn Them* (1524), he explains his commitment to religious toleration.

> It follows now that the inquisitors are the greatest heretics of all, because counter to the teaching and example of Jesus they condemn heretics to fire; and before it is time, they pull up the wheat together with the tares.
>
> For Christ did not come to slaughter, kill, burn, but so that those who live should live yet more abundantly. Yea, we should pray and hope for repentance as long as a person lives in this misery. But a Turk or a heretic cannot be overcome by our doing, neither by sword nor by

fire, but alone with patience and supplication, whereby we patiently await divine judgement.[3]

No religious commitment could be genuine and honoring to God if it was coerced. For the Anabaptists, the proper tool for bringing people to faith was not torture or imprisonment, but patience and prayer.

Discussion Questions

1. The Anabaptists argued for the freedom to believe without violence or coercion. Is it possible to advocate for our own religious freedom but refuse that same freedom to others? Have you seen that in your own life or in the world around you?

2. Hubmaier believed that religious freedom should be extended to people who he strongly disagreed with – including those of other faiths. Take a moment to think of a group of people who you disagree strongly with. How far would you go to defend their freedoms?

---

[3] Balthasar Hubmaier, "On Heretics and Those Who Burn Them (1524)," in *Balthasar Hubmaier, Theologian of Anabaptism*, ed. H. Wayne Pipkin and John Howard Yoder, *Classics of the Radical Reformation* (Scottdale, Pa.; Kitchener, ON: Herald Press, 1989), 62.

Prayer

Lord, you came to give us abundant life. You call us to live in freedom and to proclaim the gospel freely to others. Give me the strength to boldly share the good news with others in word and in deed. When I disagree with others, help me to show patience and love.

Amen

Day 2
Freedom to Disagree
(Paul Glock)

As you sent me into the world, I have sent them into the world. For them I sanctify myself, that they too may be truly sanctified. My prayer is not for them alone. I pray also for those who will believe in me through their message, that all of them may be one, Father, just as you are in me and I am in you. May they also be in us so that the world may believe that you have sent me. —John 17:18-21

During their lengthy imprisonment in a castle near Stuttgart between 1558 and 1576, Anabaptist leaders Paul Glock and Adam Horneck were repeatedly questioned and tortured by their captors. Not only did Glock and Horneck defend their beliefs, but they questioned the right of their Christian captors to jail and torture them. After quoting the above passage from John 17, Glock and Horneck argued that Christians should not attempt to force the beliefs of others.

> Now, my dear man (we said to the priest), where did God command his Son and tell him: 'Go, my son Christ, into all the world, for I am putting my word into your mouth

and have anointed you. Teach all people, but those who will not believe your teaching and preaching nor accept it, you shall capture and torture. You are to torment them until they believe what I told them and what you preached.'[4]

Sixteenth-century Anabaptists developed their convictions in an era of state-sponsored violence against minorities. Across Europe, Anabaptists were persecuted by all types of nominally Christian governments. One of the most perplexing ethical dilemmas that they faced was the reality that Christians in positions of power tortured and killed other Christians who they disagreed with.

Glock and Horneck protested that this was contrary to the New Testament, where the Father sent Christ into the world and invited people to freely respond to the gospel. Christian leaders who used force to make others change their beliefs showed that Christ did not send them.

---

[4] Paul Glock, "First Defense (1563)," in *Sources of South German/Austrian Anabaptism*, ed. Walter Klaassen et al., *Classics of the Radical Reformation* (Kitchener, ON: Pandora Press ; co-published with Herald Press, 2001), 317.

Discussion Questions

1. Glock and Horneck did not want to be coerced into changing their convictions, but they did try to persuade others to believe. What is the difference between coercion and persuasion?

2. In your church, family, work, or circle of relationships, how can you promote respectful conversation on difficult topics, including Christian beliefs that may be controversial?

Prayer

Lord, I am grateful that you have given me the freedom to believe. When people disagree with me about matters of faith, fill me with your grace and peace so that I might use persuasion without coercion. Help me to trust you to do the convincing by your Holy Spirit.

Amen

Day 3
The Holy Spirit and Human Initiative (Menno Simons)

Good and upright is the Lord; therefore he instructs sinners in his ways. He guides the humble in what is right and teaches them his way. —Psalm 25:8-9

One of the reasons that Anabaptists supported religious freedom was that they were optimistic about the Holy Spirit's work in human hearts. They believed that God's power and grace enabled people to renounce sin and choose faith. Human free will cooperated with the work of God. In his commentary on the twenty-fifth Psalm, Menno Simons shared part of his own testimony of how he responded to God when God reached out to him. He writes:

> You accepted me in love and converted me to a new understanding. You led me with your right hand and taught me through your Holy Spirit. Then by my own free will I began also to strive against the world, the flesh and the devil. I renounced all my comforts, serenity, honor and easy living and willingly took upon myself the

heavy cross of the Lord Jesus Christ. Now I also am an inheritor of that promised kingdom with all servants of God and disciples of Christ.[5]

Because of the revelation he had received from God, Menno was prepared to leave the comforts of his former life and risk everything to spread the Anabaptist message. For the remainder of his life, Menno was confident that God's Holy Spirit was preparing others to do the same.

Discussion Questions

1. How could a renewed confidence in the work of the Holy Spirit – between human and divine action – impact your life, your church, and the world around you?

2. How could a deeper understanding of the life and teachings of Christ motivate a change in your heart? Have you experienced such a change or seen it in the life of someone close to you?

---

[5] Menno Simons, "A Meditation on the Twenty-Fifth Psalm (1537)," in *Early Anabaptist Spirituality: Selected Writings*, ed. Daniel Liechty (New York: Paulist Press, 1994), 252.

Prayer

Lord Jesus, I believe that you are active in my world. Forgive me for sometimes putting my own mission ahead of yours. When I am unsure of what to do to serve you, open my eyes to what your Holy Spirit is already doing in me and around me. Give me the grace and strength to cooperate with your work in the world.

Amen

Day 4
Struggling with sin
(Menno Simons)

In the same way, count yourselves dead to sin but alive to God in Christ Jesus. Therefore do not let sin reign in your mortal body so that you obey its evil desires. Do not offer any part of yourself to sin as an instrument of wickedness, but rather offer yourselves to God as those who have been brought from death to life; and offer every part of yourself to him as an instrument of righteousness. For sin shall no longer be your master, because you are not under the law, but under grace. —Romans 6:11-14

Anabaptists believed that people should choose their own faith. This was initially expressed through the decision to be baptized and afterwards through steps of obedience in Christian fellowship. This confidence in the ability of people to respond to God ran the risk of underestimating both human sinfulness and God's holiness. In other words, if a Christian could achieve a significant measure of holiness on earth due to personal effort, what was the need for the grace of God?

This challenge was not lost on Anabaptist leaders like Menno Simons, who attempted to balance human effort and divine grace. He writes:

We are not cleansed in baptism of our inherited sinful nature, which is in our flesh, so that it is entirely destroyed in us, for it remains with us after baptism. But since the merciful Father, from whom descend all good and perfect gifts, has graciously given us the most holy faith, through His holy Word; therefore we declare in the baptism we receive that we desire to die unto the inherent, sinful nature, and destroy it, so that it will no longer be master in our mortal bodies [Romans 6:12], even though such true believers are often overcome by sin.[6]

For Menno, when a person sincerely believed the good news of grace, peace, mercy, and the forgiveness of sins proclaimed in the gospel, the positive steps of obedience that followed were a cooperative venture with God, since the power of God was released by faith. Although Christians could still be overcome by sin, they were free from the power of sin. As an almost natural consequence, believers who experienced true conversion would demonstrate signs of godly character and acts of obedience, such as baptism. These fruits were brought forth in the believer's life by the power of the Holy Spirit.

---

[6] Simons, "Christian Baptism (1539)," in *The Complete Writings of Menno Simons, C. 1496-1561*, 245.

Discussion Questions

1. What can happen when Christians forget that the goodness or holiness that they may have achieved is also a result of the grace of God in their lives?

2. Can you describe an experience where the grace of God enabled you better to respond to God in obedience and faithfulness?

Prayer

Lord Jesus, please forgive me when I have believed that my weakness was beyond your grace or when I have taken credit for the good character and good behavior that you have produced in my life. I want to respond to your grace out of gratitude for all that you have done for me. You have saved me by your grace. In your grace I wish to remain.

Amen

Day 5
Choosing Baptism
(Menno Simons)

Then Jesus came to them and said, "All authority in heaven and on earth has been given to me. Therefore go and make disciples of all nations, baptizing them in the name of the Father and of the Son and of the Holy Spirit, and teaching them to obey everything I have commanded you. And surely I am with you always, to the very end of the age."
—Matthew 28:18-20

The importance of Matthew 28: 18-20 for the Anabaptists cannot be overemphasized. Often supported by Mark 16:16, it was the central text supporting their separation from the Catholic, Reformed, and Lutheran churches. Anabaptists made their stand on believer's baptism and were persecuted for this departure from the state-supported churches. When the Anabaptists read the final words of Christ in Matthew 28, they insisted that the preaching and teaching of the gospel had to precede baptism. For them infant baptism was backwards because true baptism could occur only *after* listeners had heard the gospel and made a personal decision to believe. Menno Simons writes,

> Here we have the Lord's commandment concerning baptism, as to when according to the ordinance of God it shall be administered and received; namely, that the Gospel must first be preached, and then those baptized who believe it, as Christ says.[7]

Not only did this understanding exclude infants from baptism, but it also laid the foundation for the Anabaptist church, since higher standards of conduct could be expected of those who had willingly chosen to follow Christ and who willingly entered into Christian community.

Discussion Questions

1. In your own life, what is the connection between belief and baptism? Does belief lead to baptism, or the opposite, or both?

2. Should higher standards of conduct be expected of those who choose baptism as adults? What should those standards be?

---

[7] Simons, "Foundation of Christian Doctrine (1539)," in *The Complete Writings of Menno Simons, C. 1496-1561*, 120.

Prayer

Thank you, Lord Jesus, for calling me to faith and for the privilege of being your witness in the world. Help me to step forward in obedience with whatever act of discipleship you have prepared for me today.

Amen

Day 6
Faith for the Common Person
(Hans Schlaffer)

Then he opened their minds so they could understand the Scriptures. He told them, "This is what is written: The Messiah will suffer and rise from the dead on the third day, and repentance for the forgiveness of sins will be preached in his name to all nations, beginning at Jerusalem. You are witnesses of these things."
—Luke 24:45-48

Much of sixteenth-century Anabaptist theology was permeated by the idea that God gave people both the ability and the responsibility to follow Christ. Believers could not inherit the faith of their parents. Rulers could not decide the faith or church of their subjects. Instead, Anabaptists preached that true Christians had to decide to follow Christ, be baptized as believers, and choose their own church.

Under the influence of Martin Luther's writings, Hans Schlaffer left the Catholic priesthood in 1526 and became an Anabaptist leader in Austria. In a tract published the following year, he explained how accessible the gospel was to everyone.

> The Father teaches, seeks and wills that all people will be saved, for he teaches and seeks all people. When a good-hearted person is instructed in the truth through all creatures, through the scriptures and through the teachings, life and example of Christ, he finds in his heart that this way and no other leads to salvation. Nor can there be another way. This is confirmed in his heart. The gospel of all creatures is preached to him and he is instructed and made a disciple. To him repentance and forgiveness of sins in the name of Christ are proclaimed.[8]

For Hans, the common person did not need to defer to university scholars, priests, or princes in matters of faith. Regardless of whether one was a peasant, merchant, or ruler, what really mattered was having a heart open to the witness of God as shown in creation, in the Bible, and in the example and teachings of Christ. True disciples believed the message of repentance and forgiveness of sins that Christ preached, even if it meant a life of hardship and suffering for them. Schlaffer was captured by the authorities and executed in 1528.

---

[8] Schlaffer, "Instruction on Beginning a True Christian Life (1527)," in *Early Anabaptist Spirituality: Selected Writings*, 105.

Discussion Questions

1. Do 'common people' have an advantage when it comes to living a sincere and committed Christian life? How do wealth and power make discipleship more difficult?

2. Schlaffer believed that God communicated the gospel message through creation, the Bible, and the life of Christ. How have each of these been important in your faith journey?

Prayer

Holy Father, forgive me for the times when I have ignored your voice as you spoke to me through your created world, through the Bible or through the life and teachings of Christ. Help me also to hear you as you speak to me through the people around me. I am in awe and overwhelmed that you would give me – a flawed and broken person – an invitation to believe and to follow in your footsteps.
Thank you.

Amen

Part II
Following Christ
(Discipleship)

For Anabaptists, the personal faith that led to baptism was the starting point of a journey of discipleship. The words and teachings of Jesus were a primary subject of reflection, especially the Sermon on the Mount (Matthew 5-7). They took the Bible seriously and sought to obey it, even when it brought them into conflict with state or religious authorities. Like other Christians of the sixteenth century, their practice of discipleship was inspired by a belief in the Second Coming of Christ. They wanted to give a good account of their lives to their Lord when he returned to judge the earth and take home his church.

To evade the authorities, they often preached the Anabaptist message in forests, remote locations, and had secret meetings in homes. In another important departure from the state-sponsored Christianity of the time, the Anabaptists recruited ordinary and sometimes un-educated people not only as converts but also as leaders of the movement. All believers were invited to follow Christ and serve the community according to their gifts and talents. Out of this message of personal responsibility and opportunity, a broadly-based movement of evangelism and discipleship emerged, where farmers, artisans and the educated proclaimed the Christian message to their friends and neighbors in a spirit of loving invitation rather than force or coercion.

> O loving Father, we publicly confess that your fatherly will is not being done in us earthly humans, for our will is fully and completely in contradiction to your divine will. We pray you to send us your Holy Spirit, that he might work in us genuine faith, constant hope, and fervent love, that we might make our will in all things to be subject to your fatherly will.[9]
>
> Balthasar Hubmaier,
> *A Brief 'Our Father'* (1526)

---

[9] Balthasar Hubmaier, "A Brief 'Our Father' (1526)," in *Balthasar Hubmaier, Theologian of Anabaptism*, ed. H. Wayne Pipkin and John Howard Yoder, *Classics of the Radical Reformation* (Scottdale, Pa.; Kitchener, ON: Herald Press, 1989), 242. For the ease of contemporary readers, 'you' is substituted for 'thee' and 'thou' in this quote.

Day 7
The Primacy of Scripture (Menno Simons)

I am astonished that you are so quickly deserting the one who called you to live in the grace of Christ and are turning to a different gospel — which is really no gospel at all. Evidently some people are throwing you into confusion and are trying to pervert the gospel of Christ. But even if we or an angel from heaven should preach a gospel other than the one we preached to you, let them be under God's curse!
—Galatians 1:6-8

Anabaptist approaches to Scripture produced innovative interpretations of Christian discipleship and a new kind of church life. For Anabaptists, no church tradition, political arrangement, or social expectation could take precedence over their commitment to follow Christ on the path of discipleship. Concerning infant baptism, Menno Simons wrote in his *Foundation of Christian Doctrine*,

> I admonish and advise you if you seek God with all your heart, and do not want to be deceived, do not depend upon men and the doctrine of men no matter how venerable, holy, and

excelent they may be esteemed. For the experts, ancient as well as modern, are opposed to each other. Put your trust in Christ alone and in His Word, and in the sure instruction and practice of His holy apostles, and by the grace of God you will be safe from all false doctrine and the power of the devil, and will walk with a free and pious mind before God.[10]

In other words, believers were called to discover God's Word for themselves and put it into practice in their lives. Anabaptist readings of the Bible paid close attention to the life of Christ, often accepting the commands of Jesus at face value. They believed that a prerequisite to understanding a biblical text was a willingness to obey it. For them, interminable discussions about the meaning of texts were irrelevant if the believer was not willing to apply it in everyday life.

Discussion Questions

1. What are the benefits or risks of relying on others for our understanding of the Bible? What problems arise from relying only on ourselves or a small group of people when reading the Bible?

---

[10] Simons, "Foundation of Christian Doctrine (1539)," in *The Complete Writings of Menno Simons, C. 1496-1561*, 138.

2. Can you remember times when a text from the Bible inspired you to take a particular course of action?

Prayer

Heavenly Father, I want to confess that sometimes I struggle to understand your Word. Please help me to live in the grace of Christ, be free from false beliefs, walk in freedom and bear fruit. I desire to hear your voice, develop convictions that honor you, and listen to wise counsel. I want to trust in you and in your Word.

Amen

Day 8
Christ's Return and Discipleship (Hans Denck)

Now, brothers and sisters, about times and dates we do not need to write to you, for you know very well that the day of the Lord will come like a thief in the night. While people are saying, "Peace and safety," destruction will come on them suddenly, as labor pains on a pregnant woman, and they will not escape. But you, brothers and sisters, are not in darkness so that this day should surprise you like a thief.
—1 Thessalonians 5:1-4

The second coming of Christ was a shared conviction of all Christians in the sixteenth century. For Anabaptists, the belief that Jesus was coming back for his church encouraged believers to live holy lives. The apocalyptic End of the Age was bad news for those who had not been faithful to Christ. But for the faithful, the anticipated reign of Christ was good news.

Even Hans Denck – whose contemplative spirituality was perhaps less prone to biblical literalism than other Anabaptists – did not neglect to remind his followers to prepare a future when they would be held responsible for their lives before Christ. He wrote,

> All who truly fear God must renounce the world. And in the measure that they have to use the world out of necessity, they ought always to be prepared for struggle and ready for adversity as sojourners upon the earth. Whoever lives in security and happiness in the world should take care lest he be overtaken with her … For the Lord is coming. He will come at night, when none will take note of him, like a thief.[11]

For Denck, Christians should not think that they could name Christ as king without accepting his rule in their lives. They should not be too sure of their own goodness, for that would just make it harder for them at Christ's judgment. Instead, their faith should be shown by obedience to the rule of love. With humble hearts, they should seek the grace and forgiveness of God. Although there have been many different interpretations over the centuries, the return of Christ is a core belief of the Christian faith. It emerged from the Bible and is present in the earliest creeds.

---

[11] Hans Denck, "Whether God Is the Cause of Evil (1526)," in *Spiritual and Anabaptist Writers*, ed. George Huntston Williams, Angel M. Mergal, and Juan de Valdés (Philadelphia: Westminster Press, 1957), 106.

Discussion Questions

1. Does the doctrine of the return of Christ make you fearful or hopeful? Does it inspire you to greater faithfulness and obedience to God?

2. What behavior or attitudes - both good and bad - might characterize Christians if they really believed that Jesus could return 'like a thief in the night'?

Prayer

Thank you, Father, for your mercy and power which lead me to faith and holiness. Help me to examine myself so that I can prepare myself for your return, whenever that may be and however it may come to pass.

Amen

Day 9
Radical Obedience
(Balthasar Hubmaier)

Jesus came to Simon Peter, who said to him, "Lord, are you going to wash my feet?" Jesus replied, "You do not realize now what I am doing, but later you will understand." "No," said Peter, "you shall never wash my feet." Jesus answered, "Unless I wash you, you have no part with me." "Then, Lord," Simon Peter replied, "not just my feet but my hands and my head as well!" —John 13:6-9

The Anabaptists were very serious about obeying the Bible. They fervently sought to put the Bible into practice even when their opponents asserted that their zeal was unnecessary, or that their actions were disruptive to society. Balthasar Hubmaier argued that because God expected the Israelites to obey 'trifling' commands, Christians should take most seriously Jesus' instructions regarding baptism.

> Sometimes God demands from us the most trifling and most unattractive works in order to test us and to cast down our worldly wisdom. Was it not a simple work which he demanded from Adam and Eve that they should not eat

from the fruit of precisely that tree? ... Foot washing was not too modest either, was it? And yet Christ said to Peter, "If I do not wash you, you will have no part in me." Well, dear friends, even though in the eyes of human beings these works are low, still God wants them.[12]

Although they consistently interpreted obscure or difficult passages through the life and witness of Christ, the Anabaptists were accused of going overboard with their extreme observance of biblical commands. Nevertheless, it was precisely this radical discipleship that fueled the growth of the Anabaptist movement, prompting new missionary callings, and creating new communities of faith.

Discussion Questions

1. What is your approach to understanding the Bible and having your life shaped by it?

2. If your church was overcome by a spirit of radical obedience, would it excite you or concern you?

---

[12] Hubmaier, "On the Christian Baptism of Believers (1525)," in *Balthasar Hubmaier, Theologian of Anabaptism*, 126.

Prayer

Lord, I thank you for your word, which guides me in truth and righteousness. Help me to take it seriously, to understand it rightly, and to live it faithfully.

Amen

Day 10
Standing Firm
(Martyrs Mirror)

Then you will be handed over to be persecuted and put to death, and you will be hated by all nations because of me. At that time many will turn away from the faith and will betray and hate each other, and many false prophets will appear and deceive many people. Because of the increase of wickedness, the love of most will grow cold, but the one who stands firm to the end will be saved. And this gospel of the kingdom will be preached in the whole world as a testimony to all nations, and then the end will come.
—Matthew 24:9-13

In the sixteenth century, receiving believer's baptism indicated a serious and severe break with both religious and state authorities. When the Anabaptists were captured, a quick release was often obtained by renouncing their adult baptism and making vows of loyalty to the state and to the established church. But some Anabaptists chose to suffer and die for their new faith even when they had the opportunity to flee.

In 1533, Christina Haring was captured in Kitzbuehl, Austria, but because she was pregnant and the child's birth was imminent, the authorities consented to release her until the child was born. *The Martyrs Mirror*, an important Anabaptist history of martyrs, recounts,

> Although she knew that she would be apprehended again, and might have escaped ten times, or even more, she did not flee, but boldly remained. When she saw the officer coming, she went out to meet him, and asked him what he desired. He said: 'I have come to take you away again;' and thus they again took her to the town of Kitzbuehl, where shortly afterwards she was executed with the sword (which is not usually done with a woman), for the faith to which she steadfastly adhered. Her body was afterwards burnt.[13]

Christina paid a high price for her refusal to turn away from her Anabaptist faith. Her newborn child did, too. Like many Christians before and since, she sought to remain faithful to Christ in the most trying of circumstances.

---

[13] Thieleman J. van Braght, *The Bloody Theatre or Martyr's Mirror of the Defenceless Christians Who Baptized Only Upon Confession of Faith, and Who Suffered and Died for the Testimony of Jesus, Their Savior, from the Time of Christ to the Year A.D. 1600*, 28 ed. (Scottsdale, Pa.: Herald Press, 2007), 441.

Discussion Questions

1. Have you or someone you know ever had to face dire consequences for remaining faithful to Christ? Do you agree with everyone who believes that they are persecuted?

2. What does it mean for you to 'stand firm until the end'?

Prayer

Lord Jesus, it is sometimes difficult for me to accept the consequences for even my own poor behavior. It is even more difficult to be punished for standing firm in my faith. Help me to be discerning and know when to take a stand, and when I do, help me to remain faithful.

Amen

Day 11
Keeping your Word when it Hurts (Paul Glock)

But thanks be to God, who always leads us as captives in Christ's triumphal procession and uses us to spread the aroma of the knowledge of him everywhere. For we are to God the pleasing aroma of Christ among those who are being saved and those who are perishing. To the one we are an aroma that brings death; to the other, an aroma that brings life. And who is equal to such a task? Unlike so many, we do not peddle the word of God for profit. On the contrary, in Christ we speak before God with sincerity, as those sent from God. —2 Corinthians 2:14-17

The Hutterite missionary Paul Glock knew the importance of good Christian conduct and the impact of a holy life. He was imprisoned near Stuttgart between 1558 and 1573 under various conditions which were largely dependent on his relationship with the prison warden. For a period of six months in 1566 he had secured the considerable confidence of the prison warden, who left Glock's cell unlocked and used him as a personal messenger. Glock functioned essentially as a free man and was able to earn extra money for himself during his errands! He only had to promise to return to his cell after each assignment, which he did. Paul made use of his time outside the prison to witness.

Eventually, after Glock and a fellow Hutterite prisoner helped put out a fire in the prison, he was released and given a travelling allowance to make the journey to Moravia, in the present-day Czech Republic. During his imprisonment, Paul wrote to his wife Else,

> Why then should we, too, not wish to be a sweet odor of Christ to both the devout and the godless? For to those who are saved this is a sweet odor to life, and to those who are lost it is a testimony, so that they may have no excuse. For never may the truth be better attested to and sealed than with the blood of the saints.[14]

Throughout his time in prison, and during the brief periods of liberty that he enjoyed before his release, Paul sought to win to faith all who he could through his word and good conduct. Each day many Christians face the struggle of honoring God when doing so puts them at a disadvantage. Glock shows us that God can use our integrity as an

---

[14] Glock, "Letter to His Wife Else (1563)," in *Sources of South German/Austrian Anabaptism*, 299.

invitation to others to follow him. Our lives can be an aroma of Christ to the world.

Discussion Questions

1. When Glock returned to the prison each day instead of escaping, what kind of responses might he have received from his fellow prisoners?

2. Can you think of an example where Christian witness took on a bad odor because of bad behavior? Or where good Christian conduct paved the way for greater witness? Are there times when the line between good and bad behavior has become blurry for you?

Prayer (from Paul Glock, 1563)

> May the Lord guide your hearts and ours according to the image of Christ, our redeemer, so that we may be formed like him more and more completely. May the life of Christ in us be a mirror to the world and may we and all the devout eternally take comfort in it. May the true son, Jesus Christ, grant this.
>
> Amen.[15]

---

[15] Glock, "Letter to his Wife Else (1563)," 308.

Day 12
Faith under Pressure
(Hans Schmidt)

So we say with confidence,
"The Lord is my helper; I will not be afraid.
What can mere mortals do to me?
—Hebrews 13:6

In 1590, Hans Schmidt was jailed for his Anabaptist convictions and interrogated under torture. However, Schmidt did not respond to this poor treatment in a way that his interrogators expected. Instead, he developed a reputation among his fellow prisoners as an upright and honest man. When the authorities asked one of his cellmates – a mercenary accused of murder – what Hans was doing, he answered, "Hans prays and I curse; thus we are even." Later, the mercenary pleaded for Hans based on his good conduct.

> The overseer and the others had gone to the prison and asked the mercenary, 'My dear man, they are torturing Hans severely and racking him. What does he say when he is with you?' He [the mercenary] said 'Why do you torment the poor devil? I can see nothing wrong in him except that he prays day and night. He says he

has the right religion and will not depart from it.'[16]

With intercession from his father, Hans was released four months after his capture and banished from the country. In his extreme hardship, Hans could have concluded that God had abandoned him and said whatever was necessary to secure his release. Instead, he remained firm in his faith and was able to witness to the faithfulness of God.

Discussion Questions

1. What kind of extraordinary challenges to your faith have you faced? Even if they did not come to torture, how did these extreme experiences shape and form your faith?

2. In such times, what has helped you to remain faithful to God? How did you struggle to be faithful?

---

[16] Hans Schmidt, "Hans Schmidt's Experiences in Württemberg (1590)," in *Sources of South German/Austrian Anabaptism*, ed. Walter Klaassen et al., *Classics of the Radical Reformation* (Kitchener, ON: Pandora Press ; co-published with Herald Press, 2001), 377.

Prayer

Father, I am deeply grateful for the freedoms and blessings that I experience, and for the family and friends who support and encourage me. When I pass through a season of trial, give me the strength to remain faithful to you, even as I wait for your deliverance. Open my eyes to those who are suffering for their convictions. Give them grace and help me to be a friend to them.

Amen

Part III
Christian Community (Church)

The Anabaptist vision of Christian discipleship emphasized voluntary participation in a local Christian community – a process that was initiated through the practice of believer's baptism. Anabaptist believers within these communities sought to hold one another accountable to high standards of Christian conduct. Anabaptist assemblies were meant to be redemptive for all those who participated – places where Christian love and support could be encouraged, and where personal holiness was nurtured.

Anabaptists were not prepared to accept a regional church composed of both committed disciples and others bound to the church through social convention, family commitment, or political ambition. Instead, the Anabaptist churches were united by personal conversion, believer's baptism, the community of goods, and church discipline.

All the Anabaptist teachers and missionaries in this section sought the restoration of the church to the doctrines and practices of the early church as they understood them from the New Testament. These practices included the radical sharing of possessions, church discipline, and restoration.

Once new converts had demonstrated both sound doctrine and holy living, they could be sent forth to share the good news with others.

> O eternal Father, we pray for all the brothers and sisters. Keep them steadfast in your divine name, that they may be able to keep your commandments, unwavering until the end, able to drink fully that cup which you have given us. We pray also for all lords, princes and people in authority. Enlighten them in your divine truth, that they use the power you have given them to protect the good and punish the wicked. And stay their hand from the shedding of innocent blood. [17]

Hans Schlaffer
Two Prayers (1527)

---

[17] Schlaffer, "Two Prayers (1527)," in *Early Anabaptist Spirituality: Selected Writings*, 109-10.

Day 13
Saying 'Our Father' means Sharing
(Ambrosius Spittelmaier)

This, then, is how you should pray:
Our Father in heaven, hallowed be your name,
your kingdom come, your will be done,
on earth as it is in heaven.
Give us today our daily bread.
And forgive us our debts,
as we also have forgiven our debtors.
And lead us not into temptation,
but deliver us from the evil one.
—Matthew 6:9-13

The social and economic inequality of the sixteenth century prompted Anabaptist evangelists to read well-known Scripture passages in new ways. One of these early Anabaptist preachers was Ambrosius Spittelmaier, who read in the Lord's Prayer a clear challenge against all forms of selfish materialism. For Spittelmaier, true Christians could not say "Our Father" if they were not willing to share their possessions. He wrote,

He cannot say: 'This house is mine, that field is mine, this penny is mine; rather, it is all ours.' As we say, 'Our Father.' To sum up, a Christian is to claim nothing as his own, but is to have all things in common with his brother so as not to allow him to suffer need. I am not to work so that my house may be full, that my storeroom is full of meat, but am to look also at what my brother needs. A Christian looks more to his neighbor than to himself.[18]

The importance of sharing wealth with the less fortunate was a common Anabaptist theme that took various forms among Dutch, Swiss, and South German Anabaptists. They knew that what we do with our money says a great deal about our faith, often reflecting who and what we worship and find worthy (Matthew 6:21). For so many Christians, generosity is one of the toughest parts of following Jesus. And yet it can bring the greatest blessings to both the giver and receiver, and draw both into communion with each other and with God.

---

[18] Ambrosius Spitelmaier, "Questions and Answers of Ambrosius Spitelmaier (1527)," in *Sources of South German/Austrian Anabaptism*, ed. Walter Klaassen et al., *Classics of the Radical Reformation* (Kitchener, ON: Pandora Press ; co-published with Herald Press, 2001), 56.

Discussion Questions

1. Following the example of how Ambrosius Spittelmaier, reread the Lord's Prayer in Matthew 6 from an economic perspective. Can you think of ways that you or your church could be more generous with those who are in need?

2. As giver or receiver, have you ever experienced a greater communion with God that resulted from generosity?

Prayer

Father, I fall easily into the trap of thinking that all that I have is mine, that I earned it, and that I deserve it. And still I want more. Yet I know that all of my possessions ultimately come from your hand. May your kingdom come in my heart so that I may have renewed compassion and generosity for those in my church, my community, and around the world.

Amen

Day 14
New Monasticism
(Menno Simons)

Whoever says "I know him" but does not keep his commandments is a liar, and the truth is not in him, but whoever keeps his word, in him truly the love of God is perfected. By this we may know that we are in him: whoever says he abides in him ought to walk in the same way in which he walked. —1 John 2:4-6

While they disagreed on some of the implications of what it meant to follow Jesus, all Anabaptists believed that Christian communities should be characterized by good works. This emphasis on outward and collective demonstrations of personal faith led to the accusation that they were returning to Catholic monasticism. Menno Simons rejected this claim. For him, the beliefs and behaviors of Anabaptists simply demonstrated that they behaved like all true followers of Christ should.

> We trust in the grace and mercy of the Lord that we are children of God and disciples of Christ. We know no other Abbot than Him on whom all true Christians call in spirit and truth and say, Abba, Father. Our head or prior is Christ Jesus. Our procurator or purser and dispenser

who distributes His gifts to everyone is the Holy Spirit. Our profession is the sincere, frank, and fearless confession of faith. Our statues and laws are the express commandments of the Lord. Our cap and cloak are the garments of righteousness with which we would gladly clothe ourselves. Our cloisters are the assembly of the saints, the city of the living God, the heavenly Jerusalem … Behold, kind reader, this is the monkhood which we confess to and practice, and none other. By the grace and power of the Lord, we also hope to abide therein unchangeably all our lives.[19]

For their Protestant critics, the Anabaptist insistence on a 'fearless confession of faith' and obedience to 'the express commandments of the Lord' were reminiscent of the rigidity of medieval Catholicism. For these critics, Anabaptist practices ran the risk of making Christians righteous through outward doctrinal commitment and good works, thereby selling short the mercy of God. As a former priest himself, Menno objected strenuously to the comparison. Nevertheless, it may be that 'new monasticism' was a fitting description of the radical discipleship advocated in

---

[19] Simons, "Reply to False Accusations (1552)," in *The Complete Writings of Menno Simons, C. 1496-1561*, 568.

and by the servant-oriented communities that the Anabaptists were trying to establish.

Discussion Questions

1. Could you compare your church to a monastery, either positively or negatively? Do you think that this image of monastic devotion has any place in the church today?

2. What are the challenges of balancing the efforts of Christian discipleship with the unmerited salvation found in the grace of God?

Prayer

Lord, I do not want to have a lopsided Christian life. Please help me to profess with my mouth a 'sincere, frank and fearless confession of faith.' At the same time, may my life show that I abide in you and seek to walk in the way that you walked.

Amen

Day 15
Church Discipline
(Ambrosius Spittelmaier)

If your brother or sister sins, go and point out their fault, just between the two of you. If they listen to you, you have won them over. But if they will not listen, take one or two others along, so that 'every matter may be established by the testimony of two or three witnesses.' If they still refuse to listen, tell it to the church; and if they refuse to listen even to the church, treat them as you would a pagan or a tax collector.
—Matthew 18:15-17

For Ambrosius Spittelmaier, spiritual conversion was empty, meaningless, and possibly even false if it was not accompanied by a willingness to engage in tough conversations where sins, weaknesses and failures were exposed to the righteousness and forgiveness of Christ. At the trial preceding his beheading in 1528, this early Anabaptist preacher was asked about the principles that guided his fellowship. He wrote,

> The union, however, and fraternity which we maintain with one another, is nothing else but this: wherever we are together we intend to maintain brotherly discipline, wherever one sees

or finds the other erring, just as Christ has commanded us. We do not separate from each other in spite of all our differences, nor does one offend the other. One is not to keep anything from the other but holds all things in common whether it be in spiritual or temporal gifts. We wish to harm no one and wish to keep our covenant between God and us as long as body and life last. Such covenanting takes place when we keep the Lord's Supper.[20]

Spittelmaier's Anabaptist community understood that when they took the Lord's Supper together, they committed themselves to a form of mutual accountability that undergirded their community. Spittelmaier rather optimistically insisted that the practice of correction never led to disagreements or separations. Matthew 18:15-20 was an important text for Anabaptists even though they struggled with its application. Nevertheless, Spittelmaier points the way to an ideal of Christian fellowship that many hope for.

---

[20] Spittelmaier, in *Sources of South German/Austrian Anabaptism*, 55.

Discussion Questions

1. Do you know of examples where church discipline produced disagreement, separation, or even violence? Was this disunity avoidable?

2. Spittelmaier asserts that mutual accountability can take place without offense. How can we keep from offending when we challenge fellow Christians on their behavior? How can we avoid being offended when we are challenged?

Prayer

Lord Jesus, as I seek to maintain high standards of Christian conduct, please give me the humility and understanding to accept direction and correction, the grace, patience, and love to have tough conversations with others, and the wisdom to understand the limits of perfectionism.

Amen

Day 16
Restoration
(The Hutterite Chronicle)

If anyone has caused grief, he has not so much grieved me as he has grieved all of you to some extent – not to put it too severely. The punishment inflicted on him by the majority is sufficient. Now instead, you ought to forgive and comfort him, so that he will not be overwhelmed by excessive sorrow. I urge you, therefore, to reaffirm your love for him.
—2 Corinthians 2:5-8

The high standards of Christian conduct that were promoted in Anabaptist communities included a practice of confronting sins according to Matthew 18:15-17. Instructions on church discipline, sometimes leading to excommunication ('the ban'), are found in the earliest Anabaptist documents, including the Schleitheim Confession of 1527. While not always successful, the main goal of confronting poor Christian behavior was not exclusion, but repentance and restoration to the community, according to the biblical example recorded in 2 Corinthians 2:5-8.

Between 1531 and 1533, several conflicts rocked the Hutterite community in Austerlitz, Moravia, which is today part of the Czech Republic. One of these involved Georg Zaunring, who was a Hutterite leader and teacher of the community. In 1531, when Georg and another leader discovered that Georg's wife had committed adultery with a man in the community, they disciplined the guilty pair privately and leniently rather than bringing it before the whole church. When the affair became public knowledge, Georg himself was removed from leadership and excluded from fellowship for keeping the matter private. In response, Georg acknowledged his fault and was welcomed back into the church, as the *Hutterite Chronicle* describes,

> Zaunring admitted his sin and said many times that his heartfelt wish was to change. He was taken back into the church with intercession to the Lord on his behalf. As his whole life continued upright, he was again entrusted with the service of the Gospel and later sent to Franconia.[21]

That the Hutterites were prepared to send a fallen (albeit restored) leader as an evangelist shows the seriousness of their willingness to reintegrate the repentant into their community. Unfortunately,

---

[21] Hutterian Brethren, *The Chronicle of the Hutterian Brethren*, 2 vols., vol. 1 (Rifton, NY: Plough Publishing House, 1987), 93-94.

Georg's missionary service was cut short when he was captured by the authorities and executed.

Discussion Questions

1. Have you ever seen a Christian leader removed from responsibility and later restored?

2. What happens when Christians fail to address words, behaviors, and actions that have a negative impact on the church and the community?

Prayer

Holy God, I thank you for the restored relationship that I have with you through Jesus Christ. I humbly come before you in my own brokenness and ask you to continue your work in me. Give me the grace to forgive others when they have hurt me or those close to me. You are the God who restores. Help me to seek the restoration of broken relationships in my life and in my church, even as I wait for you to restore all things (Acts 3:21; Revelation 21:1).

Amen

Day 17
Unbelieving Children
(Balthasar Hubmaier)

Because of you [Israelites] the Lord became angry with me [Moses] also and said, "You shall not enter it, either. But your assistant, Joshua son of Nun, will enter it. Encourage him, because he will lead Israel to inherit it. And the little ones that you said would be taken captive, your children who do not yet know good from bad – they will enter the land. I will give it to them and they will take possession of it. But as for you, turn around and set out toward the desert along the route to the Red Sea." —Deuteronomy 1:37-40

The baptism of adult believers was the cornerstone of Anabaptist church practice, universally supported among all the various Anabaptists of the sixteenth century. In contrast with the established churches they separated from (Catholic, Lutheran, and Reformed) the Anabaptists did not baptize infants. For them, since only believing adults could be baptized, children were excluded. Early in the movement, this raised the question: if children could not be baptized, were they automatically condemned by God?

In his 1525 defense of believer's baptism, Swiss Anabaptist Bathasar Hubmaier acknowledged that the Bible did not give a clear answer to the question. Nevertheless, pointing to the innocence of children as noted in Deuteronomy 1:39, he trusted that unbaptized children would be saved by the grace of God.

> Since the hand of God is not short, he does what he wills and no one is permitted to ask him, "Why do you do that?" He is Lord. He has mercy upon whomever he wills; and whomever he will, he hardens and no one can resist his will. For it is not the willing nor the running, but the mercy of God. We are his lump of clay. He can make out of us what he wills. Therefore I say, by the authority of these passages, that he can save the infants very well by grace since they know neither good nor evil.[22]

Relying on the grace of God to save unbaptized children meant that Anabaptists could continue in their commitment to the baptism of adult and consenting believers only. It did not, however, avoid the challenge to families and to the church of how to encourage children towards a personal faith commitment as they matured.

---

[22] Hubmaier, "On the Christian Baptism of Believers (1525)," in *Balthasar Hubmaier, Theologian of Anabaptism*, 140.

Discussion Questions

1. At what age can children make a personal faith decision for themselves? How are they encouraged to do so? How should they be encouraged?

2. Children growing up in Christian homes may sometimes feel that they don't have much choice in the formation of their faith convictions. How can we ensure that they do?

Prayer

Lord Jesus, you welcomed children to come to you. May my life and my church be a place of welcome for children, youth, and young adults as you extend your grace to them so that one day, they might declare that you are Lord. When I experience anxiety about the spiritual well-being of people that I love, help me to release that anxiety to you and experience your peace.

Amen

Day 18
Generosity
(The Hutterite Chronicle)

They devoted themselves to the apostles' teaching and to the fellowship, to the breaking of bread and to prayer. Everyone was filled with awe, and many wonders and miraculous signs were done by the apostles. All the believers were together and had everything in common. Selling their possessions and goods, they gave to anyone as he had need.
—Acts 2:42-45

Between 1661 and 1665, the Hutterites living in Moravia (in the modern-day Czech Republic) fell into great poverty and reached out to the Mennonites in the Netherlands for help. As the invading armies of the Ottoman Empire advanced across Europe, they had taken food and livestock from villages, usually killing peasants and burning the village as they departed. Men were killed. Women and children were captured and taken as slaves. European armies also moved through Hutterite colonies, demanding food and horses in support of their efforts. Unable to plant or harvest crops, farming communities were brought to ruin. The *Hutterite Chronicle* describes the devastation that they experienced.

> The year 1663 drew to an end with misery, terror, and death on all sides, with much heartache, groaning, and weeping. The land was laid waste, and men and cattle perished. Anything that had not been robbed was lost in other ways. The whole church was again brought into utter poverty and ruin, for they could harvest hardly any field or garden crops.[23]

These repeated trials over four years of war were more than the industrious Hutterites could manage alone. Even as a new peace agreement gave them hope for the future, they struggled to feed themselves and lacked the funds to rebuild the burned-out houses and flour mills. They wrote to the Dutch Mennonites, who lived in peace and had seen their own economic situation improve. The Dutch Mennonites soon responded generously to the request, and their demonstration of a Christian commitment to discipleship went well beyond local interests to support others in a distant land.

---

[23] Hutterian Brethren, *The Chronicle of the Hutterian Brethren*, vol. 1, 2 vols. (Rifton, N.Y. ; Ste. Agathe, Man.: Plough Publishing House, 1987), 788.

Discussion Questions

1. Has your economic situation improved over recent years? If so, is the Lord prompting you to help people in great need, perhaps even those who suffer from war or famine?

2. Have you ever been at a place of great need in your own life and received help from others? Take a moment to thank God for the generosity of those who helped you.

Prayer (adapted from the Hutterite benediction following receipt of the Mennonite gifts)

Lord, thank you for moving the hearts of people to support me when I was in need. Help me to give generously to support those who suffer. May glory, honor and praise be to you for all eternity.

Amen

Part IV
Separation (Nonresistance)

The sixteenth century was a time of great social upheaval, economic unrest, wars, and widespread persecution of minorities. Nonresistance was by no means an obvious solution for the Anabaptists. Anabaptist views against Christians committing acts of violence were shaped by their reading of the Sermon on the Mount (Matthew 5-7). In the *Schleitheim Confession* of 1527, the separation between church and world was clear. Just as light was opposed to darkness, Christians were not to participate in the affairs of government or the violence that it supported. Although some Anabaptists, such as Balthasar Hubmaier, sought to find a middle ground, this did not last, and pacifism (or nonresistance) emerged as a spiritual conviction shared by all Anabaptists. Through their refusal to endorse violence they sought to offer a foretaste of heaven on earth, and a demonstration of divine influence in human relationships.

Forsaking arms did not mean, however, that violence was entirely absent from Anabaptist teachings. Indeed, they expected the authorities to maintain order and punish evildoers. Although they did not engage in violence themselves, they trusted God to judge the wicked. They believed that when Jesus returned, he would judge the living and the dead, including those who had persecuted them. Until that time, Anabaptist communities committed themselves to peace, the pursuit of holiness, and witness.

> O Almighty, eternal, merciful God! We give you praise and thanksgiving that you have chosen us to be your children and have opened up to us the mysteries of the divine will. For you have hidden these things from the wise of this world, O Father, according to your pleasure. We ask you to make us able to drink fully the cup you have placed before us. We pray for all those in authority in this world, that you enable them to use the sword that you have given them for the protection of the good and punishment of evil. Watch over them, so that they do not mingle their hand in the blood of your saints. And give us the strength to accomplish your divine will. We pray for all the brothers and sisters who are in prison or suffering affliction and disgrace. Strengthen them according to your divine will. Amen.[24]

Hans Schlaffer
Two Prayers (1527)

---

[24] Schlaffer, "Two Prayers (1527)," in *Early Anabaptist Spirituality: Selected Writings*, 109.

Day 19
Rejecting violence (The Schleitheim Confession)

"You have heard that it was said, 'Eye for eye, and tooth for tooth.' But I tell you, do not resist an evil person. If anyone slaps you on the right cheek, turn to them the other cheek also. And if anyone wants to sue you and take your shirt, hand over your coat as well. If anyone forces you to go one mile, go with them two miles. Give to the one who asks you, and do not turn away from the one who wants to borrow from you. —Matthew 5:38-42

Early Anabaptism quickly developed a consensus that Christians were to avoid violence at all costs. The Anabaptists had experienced state-sponsored persecution firsthand and understood how Christians in government could be corrupted by power and compelled to use state resources to act in ways that would be displeasing to Christ. While governments could punish the wicked and protect the righteous, violence was "outside the perfection of Christ," and not appropriate for Christians. Instead, the *Schleitheim Confession* of 1527 urged believers to confront the evil of this world with spiritual weapons.

> Thereby shall also fall away from us the diabolical weapons of violence – such as sword, armor, and the like, and all of their use to protect friends or against enemies – by virtue of the word of Christ: 'you shall not resist evil'.[25]

Like the early Anabaptists, we live in a violent world, encompassing many kinds of violence: domestic, religious, racial, ethnic, national, and international (to name but a few). In each violent incident there are perpetrators and victims. Cycles of violence – sometimes instigated or maintained by governments, and sometimes by individuals – can drag families, communities, and countries into a devil's playground of hatred, pain, and oppression. As it was then, so it is now. The word of Christ can bring wholeness, repentance, reconciliation, and repentance.

---

[25] *The Schleitheim Confession (1527)*, ed. John Howard Yoder (Scottdale, Pa.: Herald Press, 1977), 13.

Discussion Questions

1. We can be tempted to call attention to the violence of others and ignore the violence in our own hearts. Is there a relationship where you have been angry or aggressive where you need to seek the peace of Christ?

2. Have you been a victim in an unhealthy cycle of violence? Do you need to take action to separate yourself from evil?

Prayer

Lord, it is hard for me to turn the other cheek when I have been wronged. It is easy for me to turn a blind eye to the violence around me. Give me the spiritual strength to choose neither passivity nor violence, but to share the peace of Christ around me.

Amen

Day 20
Separation of Church and State (The Schleitheim Confession)

After the people saw the sign Jesus performed, they began to say, "Surely this is the Prophet who is to come into the world." Jesus, knowing that they intended to come and make him king by force, withdrew again to a mountain by himself. —John 6:14-15

The Anabaptist commitment to non-violence and the concurrent belief in a firm separation of church and state meant that Anabaptist teachers routinely stressed that Christians should not only reject military service, but government positions as well. For them, the spiritual realm of the church and the earthly mandate of governments were separate. And while they understood that there could be short-term benefits to collaboration between church and state, they observed that these were uneven partnerships that usually led to the division or corruption of the church.

Third, is asked concerning the sword: whether the Christian should be a magistrate if he is chosen thereto. This is answered thus: Christ was to be made king, but He fled and did not discern the ordinance of His Father. Thus we should also do as He did and follow after Him, and we should not walk in darkness. For He Himself says: "Whoever would come after me, let him deny himself and take up his cross and follow me."[26]

According to the *Schleitheim Confession* (1527), believers in Christ were to deny themselves (Matthew 16:24), follow his example and flee the invitation to associate themselves with secular governments (John 6:15). This meant that a Christian could not be a ruler, a judge, or serve in the military or police without compromising the faith. Christians had spiritual weapons, but they were not to support or participate in acts of violence.

Today, many Anabaptists whose historical convictions involved absolute non-involvement in the political sphere have experienced new opportunities for engagements with governments that are not bent on punishing them for their beliefs. In other countries, Christians and other religious minorities continue to experience violent

---

[26] *The Schleitheim Confession (1527)*, 15. Matthew 16:24.

persecution. In both situations, early Anabaptists remind us that we cannot ignore the complex tensions that exist between faith and politics.

Discussion Questions

1. What should Christians do when their government encourages them to perform good deeds?

2. Have you ever needed to separate from social or political responsibilities in order to preserve your faith?

Prayer

Lord Jesus, I want to live a holy life, following your example of sacrifice and peace in a broken and fallen world. I confess that I have sometimes given my loyalty to others, including governments and elected leaders, instead of you. You are my King. Please help me to give you my undivided loyalty, even when I face consequences for doing so.

Amen

Day 21
Spiritual Weapons
(Menno Simons)

For though we live in the world, we do not wage war as the world does. The weapons we fight with are not the weapons of the world. On the contrary, they have divine power to demolish strongholds. We demolish arguments and every pretension that sets itself up against the knowledge of God, and we take captive every thought to make it obedient to Christ.
—2 Corinthians 10:3-5

In the *Schleitheim Confession* and many other early Anabaptist documents, church and state were understood to be in strong opposition to each other: governments ruled according to the flesh, while Christians were led by the Spirit. The allegiance of rulers was to their cities or nations, while Christians were citizens of heaven. Governments used swords and other weapons of violence, whereas Christians sought to arm themselves with spiritual weapons.

> Our weapons are not weapons with which cities and countries may be destroyed, walls and gates broken down, and human blood shed in torrents like water. But they are weapons with which the

spiritual kingdom of the devil is destroyed and the wicked principle in man's soul is broken down, flinty hearts broken, hearts that have never been sprinkled with the heavenly dew of the Holy Word. We have and know no other weapons besides this, the Lord, knows, even if we should be torn into a thousand pieces, and if as many false witnesses rose up against us as there are spears of grass in the fields, and grains of sand upon the seashore. Once more, Christ is our fortress; patience our weapon of defense; the Word of God our sword; and our victory a courageous, firm, unfeigned faith in Jesus Christ. And iron and metal spears and swords we leave to those who, alas, regard human blood and swine's blood about alike.[27]

Menno Simons taught that followers of Christ should solve problems differently than those in the world. Instead of engaging in violence to get their way, Christians should act with patience, hope, faith in Christ, and confidence in the Bible. Christians were engaged in a spiritual battle as they confronted the forces of evil in the world and set out to convince the hearts and minds of people with the truth of God's Holy Word.

---

[27] Simons, "Foundation of Christian Doctrine (1539)," in *The Complete Writings of Menno Simons, C. 1496-1561*, 198.

Discussion Questions

1. What can happen when Christians use the weapons of this world instead of the spiritual weapons that God provides?

2. Have you experienced a victory that God provided when human methods failed?

Prayer

Lord, forgive me for sometimes resorting to the tools of this world as I confront life's challenges. I know that I can be tempted to act before I pray. Help me to secure my own faith in your power and your methods, arming myself with truth, humility, righteousness, faith, compassion, salvation, love, and the Word of God.

Amen

Day 22
Christians in Government (Balthasar Hubmaier)

Let everyone be subject to the governing authorities, for there is no authority except that which God has established. The authorities that exist have been established by God. Consequently, whoever rebels against the authority is rebelling against what God has instituted, and those who do so will bring judgment on themselves.
—Romans 13:1-2

One Anabaptist writer who disagreed with the absolute separation between the spiritual (church) and worldly (government) realms was Swiss Anabaptist Balthasar Hubmaier. On the one hand, he agreed with the Swiss Brethren that the church should be separate from the world, a gathered community of baptized believers who were mutually committed to ethical and doctrinal standards. On the other hand, he also sought cooperation between the church and state for the benefit of the church and the well-being of all citizens.

Like his Anabaptist peers, Hubmaier strongly opposed the use of violence by the government or the gathered church to enforce any religious opinion. He taught that the only way for Christians to deal with those who had different religious convictions was the ban, the expulsion from the local congregation of those who rejected the spiritual convictions or moral standards of the church. He did, however, allow that Christians could participate in the divine mandate of government to punish evildoers (Romans 13:1-6).

> If government is so unchristian that a Christian cannot use the sword, why do we help and support it then with our taxes? Are we not obligated to our neighbor, as much as to ourselves, to prevent his injury? Why do we then choose a government? Or are those in government not our neighbors? Yes, if we desire to live in peace under a heathen government, why not much more under a Christian one, since for the Christian the order of God goes more to heart than with the heathen.[28]

Hubmaier taught that until the return of Christ, Christians had a responsibility to pay taxes, pray for their rulers, and, if necessary, support government efforts to protect citizens and punish evildoers. With his pragmatic approach, he even

---

[28] Hubmaier, "On the Sword (1525)," in *Balthasar Hubmaier, Theologian of Anabaptism*, 522-23.

suggested that a Christian in government would do a better job than a non-Christian would.

Discussion Questions

1. Do Christians tend to do a better job in government than non-Christians?

2. Do you know Christians who are elected officials, civil servants, lawyers, or judges, or who serve in the police or military? Are you aware of ways that the practice of their profession challenges their faith?

Prayer

Lord, help me to be a good citizen by respecting and praying for those in authority as they seek the well-being of those they serve. I ask that you provide special grace and wisdom for Christians who serve in challenging jobs in government, in the legal system, or in the maintenance of law and order.

Amen

Day 23
Disagreeing Peacefully (Michael Sattler)

But when he, the Spirit of truth, comes, he will guide you into all the truth. He will not speak on his own; he will speak only what he hears, and he will tell you what is yet to come. He will glorify me because it is from me that he will receive what he will make known to you. —John 16:13-14

Christians can disagree for any number of reasons. In one of the first documents of the Anabaptist movement, Michael Sattler describes his understanding of the church to the Protestant Reformers in Strasbourg. In his declaration, Sattler lists twenty points that hindered him from accepting their arguments. The letter signaled the end of the collegial relationship that had existed in Strasbourg between the Protestant Reformers and the Anabaptist leaders.

Sattler's twenty points describe Anabaptist commitments to the voluntary nature of the church, believer's baptism, nonresistance, and the church as a committed fellowship distinct from the world. After discussion of Sattler's twenty points, the Anabaptist leaders and the Protestant Reformers were not able to come to agreement.

Despite their fundamental disagreement, Sattler sought to disagree in peace. He writes to the Protestant Reformers,

> Therefore, my beloved in God, I know of no comfort in all despair except to address a humble prayer to God the Father for you and for me, that He might be willing to teach us in all truth by His Spirit. Herewith I commend you to the Lord, for as I understand it, I can no longer remain here without doing a special dishonor to God; therefore I must for the sake of my conscience leave the field to the opposition. I beg you herein, that you understand this as an act of Christian humility on my part.[29]

By 'leaving the field to the opposition,' Sattler was not conceding his case. Rather, he realized that the disagreement was significant enough so that agreement would be difficult, if not impossible. Instead of continuing the fight, he withdrew. More significantly, he still called his opponents 'brothers' and prayed that each of them would grow in their understanding of the truth.

---

[29] Michael Sattler, "Parting with the Strasbourg Reformers (1526)," in *The Legacy of Michael Sattler*, ed. John Howard Yoder, *Classics of the Radical Reformation* (Scottdale, Pa.: Herald Press, 1973), 23.

Discussion Questions

1. Have you ever experienced a significant disagreement with other Christians that led to a parting of ways? Were you able to 'leave the field' in peace, as Sattler attempted to do?

2. Sattler held his ground against those who disagreed with him. He believed that God was the ultimate judge of human hearts. How could such a belief enable him to maintain a humble attitude, even in the face of strong disagreement?

Prayer

Help me, Father, to come to a right understanding of the Bible and to be true to my convictions as I interact with others and seek to be in right relationship with each person who I encounter. Give me grace in disagreement as I acknowledge that you are the only One with all the answers to our questions.

Amen

Day 24
God's justice, not ours
(Jacob Hutter)

Then will appear the sign of the Son of Man in heaven. And then all the peoples of the earth will mourn when they see the Son of Man coming on the clouds of heaven, with power and great glory. And he will send his angels with a loud trumpet call, and they will gather his elect from the four winds, from one end of the heavens to the other. —Matthew 24:30-31

Sixteenth-century Anabaptists abandoned violence and sought peaceful ways of existing in a world that was full of injustice. Often, this meant fleeing persecution to a new region or country. Following the teaching of Christ in Matthew 6, Anabaptists refused to strike back or rebel against unjust treatment. However, they were not immune to the human longing for justice. They were committed to nonviolence, but they did not expect God to be nonviolent. Sixteenth-century Anabaptist authors developed a theology of God's justice associated with the Second Coming of Christ. In the end, only God could judge justly. Christians should not pretend to take His place, even at the hands of those who did them harm. Referring to Matthew 24:30, Jacob Hutter wrote in 1535,

> Your King and Savior, Jesus Christ the Son of God, is coming. He will soon appear on the clouds of Heaven with hosts of angels, in great power and glory. He will take vengeance on all His foes and will redeem His chosen, saving them from their enemies and from every calamity.[30]

Instead of taking violence into their own hands, they deferred such cases to God's own judgement at the Return of Christ. Because God was not going to ignore the persecution of the church and the abuse of the weak and vulnerable, Anabaptist leaders were able to leave justice in God's hands. Such thinking was a great encouragement to those facing imprisonment, torture, execution, or those who were forced from their homes.

Discussion Questions

1. How do you feel about God punishing the wicked, either in this life or the next?

2. Can a belief in God's righteous judgment be an encouragement to a Christian who has been a victim of violence, oppression, or abuse?

---

[30] Jakob Hutter, "Letter 7 (1535)," in *Brotherly Faithfulness: Epistles from a Time of Persecution*, Anabaptist Texts in Translation (Rifton, N.Y.: Plough Pub. House, 2006), 131-32.

Prayer

Forgive me, Lord, when I have desired to make my own justice by punishing, through my actions and attitudes, those who have hurt me. I acknowledge that you are the perfect Judge, and not me. Help me to live faithfully and peacefully until you return to make all things right.

Amen

Part V
Witness
(Mission)

Although they were confronted with persecution and hardship wherever they went, Anabaptist churches multiplied across medieval Europe. Their program of evangelism was based on an appeal of personal commitment to Christ, expressed through baptism, and nurtured in Christian community. Every Anabaptist believer was called to be a missionary disciple, and this created spontaneous opportunities for Christian witness among friends, family, and neighbors. Sharing one's faith was part of following Christ.

Anabaptist witness was hard, as the authors in this section illustrate. Evangelism was more than a spoken word. It was a call to a sacrificial, humble lifestyle that sometimes led to persecution and death. At the same time, words were a vital part of Anabaptist witness. Anabaptist leaders were constantly on the lookout for believers who could be trained as preachers and teachers of the Bible. These leaders would proclaim the gospel and start new churches, a task that would continue until Christ's return.

O eternal Father, we pray that you send us workers for your vineyard. For the harvest is great and the workers are few. We pray also for all missionaries sent into the world. Strengthen them with the power of your Holy Spirit. Extinguish from us all human fear so that we may proclaim your word without hesitation. Keep us in your holy name and do not allow us to turn from the spring of living water, neither in the present nor the future, high or deep, in death or in life, nor toward any other creature. Make us firm in the true faith until the end. We pray these things through your loving son Jesus Christ, who taught us to pray this in his name: Our Father in heaven, let your name be kept sacred. Let your kingdom come and your will be accomplished on earth as in heaven. Give us each day our daily bread. Forgive us our sins as we forgive those who sin against us. Keep us from temptation and deliver us from evil. For yours is the kingdom, power, and glory in eternity. Amen.[31]

Hans Schlaffer, *Two Prayers* (1527)

---

[31] Schlaffer, "Two Prayers (1527)," in *Early Anabaptist Spirituality: Selected Writings*, 110.

Day 25
Saving and Serving (Pilgram Marpeck)

Jesus called them together and said, "You know that those who are regarded as rulers of the Gentiles lord it over them, and their high officials exercise authority over them. Not so with you. Instead, whoever wants to become great among you must be your servant, and whoever wants to be first must be slave of all. For even the Son of Man did not come to be served, but to serve, and to give his life as a ransom for many."
—Mark 10:42-45

Pilgram Marpeck continued in civil service as an engineer in both Strasbourg and Augsburg after his conversion to Anabaptism. He debated with Protestant Reformers and promoted dialogue among the Swiss, South German, and Hutterite Anabaptists. In his writings, he taught that Christian witness should be accompanied by service, sacrifice, and suffering love. Following the example of Christ's earthly ministry and death, evangelism was supposed to be an incarnational demonstration of love and sacrifice to a fallen world. As a result, he was known not only for his abilities to debate and preach, but also for his professional conduct and charitable deeds.

Christ did not come to condemn or to destroy men. Nor did He come to be served. He came to offer salvation to man and, through His suffering in all patience, to save and serve them. We have been appointed by Him, not to rule over, judge, condemn, destroy, or inflict any suffering or evil on men. We are to serve them, to offer and announce to them His grace and healing, and in His name to proclaim the forgiveness of sin. Men may then be converted to their Creator, God, and Lord, repent for the forgiveness of sins, and believe in and trust God and the Lord Jesus Christ.[32]

For Marpeck, Christian preaching was not for the high and mighty filled with self-importance, but for humble servants of Christ who were active in sacrificial service.

Discussion Questions

1. Some people believe the Christian message is false because they have seen it preached by people who use their influence "to rule, judge, condemn, destroy or inflict suffering." In such situations, how can we offer God's grace and healing?

---

[32] Pilgram Marpeck, "An Epistle Concerning the Heritage and Service of Sin (1545)," in *The Writings of Pilgram Marpeck*, ed. William Klassen and Walter Klaassen, *Classics of the Radical Reformation* (Kitchener, ON; Scottdale, Pa.: Herald Press, 1978), 415-16.

2. What disciplines or habits can you nurture to promote the humble and sacrificial witness that Marpeck advocates?

Prayer

I confess, Lord, that I am easily tempted to judge and condemn others. I have even caused others to suffer. By your grace, give me the strength to follow your example as a servant so that I may announce your grace and healing to those around me.

Amen

Day 26
Witness in Word and Deed
(Ambrosius Spittelmaier)

My command is this: Love each other as I have loved you. Greater love has no one than this: to lay down one's life for one's friends. You are my friends if you do what I command. I no longer call you servants, because a servant does not know his master's business. Instead, I have called you friends, for everything that I learned from my Father I have made known to you. You did not choose me, but I chose you and appointed you so that you might go and bear fruit—fruit that will last—and so that whatever you ask in my name the Father will give you. This is my command: Love each other. —John 15:12-17

Ambrosius Spittelmaier's short-lived career as an evangelist stressed the social implications of the gospel in both the church and in society. After his arrival in a village, he would go to the tavern and ask if the gospel was preached in the local church. The ensuing discussion would often give Ambrosius a chance to discern whether his conversation partners had made a personal commitment to Christ. Then he sought to determine whether the person lived a life of committed discipleship, including the sharing of possessions with those in need. Spittelmaier elaborated on his missionary method at his trial, prior to his execution in 1528.

> When I or someone else meets someone who is not of our faith, I just ask him whether he is a Christian, what his Christian walk is, how he conducts himself towards his brother, whether he has all things in common with others and they again with him, whether any among them lack food and clothing, whether they have brotherly discipline among themselves, how they conduct themselves towards God in the use of all created things, and how they recognize God and Christ in them, etc. If one or more admit to us that they are ignorant, that they do not know, and if one desires to know, then we show him the will of God according to the trade he has.[33]

Spittelmaier's connection of personal faith with a disciplined community and with economic considerations can be understood against the background of the Peasants' War (1524-1525), a failed revolt of the poor to secure improved

---

[33] Spitelmaier, in *Sources of South German/Austrian Anabaptism*, 55.

economic and social conditions for themselves. Spittelmaier preached a message of repentance in which church discipline and care for the poor were a vital part of Christian discipleship and witness.

Discussion Questions

1. What can happen when Christian preaching or teaching neglects personal conversion, a disciplined Christian community, or care for the poor?

2. Are there Christians who have been models for you in their witness in both word and deed?

Prayer

Father, I confess that I can easily forget the love that you have for all that you have created. Help me to show your love to my family, my church, and those outside your church, in both word and deed.

Amen

Day 27
Give us this Day your Holy Word (Balthasar Hubmaier)

Father, hallowed be your name,
your kingdom come.
Give us each day our daily bread.
Forgive us our sins,
for we also forgive everyone who sins against us.
And lead us not into temptation."
—Luke 11:2-4

Do your best to present yourself to God as one approved, a worker who does not need to be ashamed and who correctly handles the word of truth.
—2 Timothy 2:15

Many Anabaptist missionaries had short careers due to persecution. At the same time, the movement was growing. There was a great and growing need for more church members to step forward in various kinds of service, especially preaching and teaching the Bible. As a result, prayers for God to raise up new workers were a regular occurrence in Anabaptist sermons and writings. Here is one from Balthasar Hubmaier, based on Luke 11:3 or Matthew 6:11.

Nourish us with the bread of your holy Word, which comes down from heaven, whereof he who eats will never hunger. Bring it to life in our soul, that it might burgeon, grow up, and bear fruit for eternal life. Give us also Christian and industrious workers, who will divide the same to us pure, clear, and undefiled and distribute it faithfully, so that your fatherly will, which can be known only from your Word, might be fulfilled.[34]

In Anabaptist prayers for workers, teachers, or missionaries, the word "faithful" comes up often. For their rapidly growing church in perilous times, Anabaptists knew that faithfulness to Christ, to Scripture, and to the community were non-negotiable qualities. They understood that while new skills could be learned and new knowledge gained, it was much more difficult to demonstrate faithfulness in tough times.

Discussion Questions

1. When you seek to fill leadership or service positions in your church, is faithfulness part of the job description? If so, how can you know that someone has been faithful?

---

[34] Hubmaier, "A Brief 'Our Father' (1526)," in *Balthasar Hubmaier, Theologian of Anabaptism*, 242-43.

2. Sixteenth-century Anabaptist leadership in church and mission work required great faithfulness because of persecution and hardships. What are the challenges faced by faithful leaders today?

Prayer

God Almighty, your Word directs me in all truth, teaches me your ways, and helps me to live a life of faithful service. As I read, study, and meditate on your Word, I pray for those who have the challenge of preaching and teaching the Scriptures today. Give them grace and strength as they seek to remain faithful.

Amen

Day 28
Transforming Witness (Menno Simons)

Turn to me and be gracious to me,
　for I am lonely and afflicted.
Relieve the troubles of my heart
　and free me from my anguish.
Look on my affliction and my distress
　and take away all my sins.
See how numerous are my enemies
　and how fiercely they hate me!
　Guard my life and rescue me;
　do not let me be put to shame,
　for I take refuge in you.
May integrity and uprightness protect me,
　because my hope, Lord, is in you.
　Deliver Israel, O God,
　from all their troubles!
—Psalm 25:16-22

In 1537, Dutch Anabaptist Menno Simons wrote a deep and heartfelt prayer to God based on Psalm 25. In it, he expressed great sorrow for his own sins before God and great concern for the church. In his comments on the last verse in the Psalm (25:22), Simons asked God to send evangelists and teachers in "these final days" to build a church that would live in peace before God and the world. He wrote,

> Create in us a chaste heart whose only desire is for your blessed word and will. Send us sincere workers for your harvest, who will reap and gather the grain at the right time. Send us faithful builders, who will lay a sure foundation so that in these final days your house may be glorious, shining above all the mountains. Then many people may come to her and say, "Come, let us go up to the mountain of the Lord, to the house of the God of Jacob. He will teach us his ways, so that we may walk in his paths" [Isaiah 2:3]. Then we may walk our whole life long before you in peace and in good conscience, under god-fearing authorities and blameless teachers, with a Christian baptism, a true supper, godly living and true separation.[35]

For God to deliver his people from their troubles, Menno believed that a faithful church required godly teachers, right doctrines, and holy living. With these in place, the world would see a separated church that is living in peace and good conscience before God.

---

[35] Simons, "A Meditation on the Twenty-Fifth Psalm (1537)," in *Early Anabaptist Spirituality: Selected Writings*, 271-72.

Discussion Questions

1. How can good teaching transform the witness of a local church?

2. Have you ever experienced such a transformation?

Prayer (modeled after Simon's prayer)

Lord, I ask that you send to my church sincere workers and faithful teachers, who can be a witness for you through their words and their good conduct. Please help me and those in my church to walk before you so that others may desire to follow you.

Amen

Day 29
Welcoming the Broken
(Jacob Hutter)

Jesus went through all the towns and villages, teaching in their synagogues, proclaiming the good news of the kingdom and healing every disease and sickness. When he saw the crowds, he had compassion on them, because they were harassed and helpless, like sheep without a shepherd. Then he said to his disciples, "The harvest is plentiful but the workers are few. Ask the Lord of the harvest, therefore, to send out workers into his harvest field."
—Matthew 9:35-38

In 1535, Jacob Hutter and the early Hutterites participated in a revival in present day Austria. The background to this spiritual awakening was economic hardship, with many families struggling with basic needs such as shelter and food. Responding to the Hutterite message of total personal and economic commitment to Christ, converts donated all their possessions to the community. In so doing, both their spiritual and material needs were met with the Hutterite all-encompassing gospel message. There was an unexpected harvest of converts. The response to their mission work was so strong that Hutter sought more missionaries to help.

> So the Almighty Father has again established His church here in Tirol [Austria] and multiplies his people daily, adding to the church those who are being saved. We have very much work to do for the Lord, day and night. As soon as we arrive at one place, we wish we could be at many other places at the same time. We need more Servants of the Word and other brothers fitted for the task and able and willing to carry out God's work. The harvest is ripe, but the workers are few.[36]

All over the world, curious people seek out Christians and churches for a variety of reasons. While there is usually some kind of spiritual interest, there may be many other personal needs as well, such as divorce, sickness, poverty, chronic unemployment, or loneliness. While new spiritual curiosity may quickly grow into a personal faith in Christ, these personal needs may not be quickly resolved. Newcomers may continue to draw more support from their new community of faith than they are able to give in return. Part of the Hutterite answer to this challenge was to require everyone to

---

[36] Hutter, "Letter 5 (1535)," in *Brotherly Faithfulness: Epistles from a Time of Persecution*, 81.

give to the church. Rich or poor, whole or broken, each new arrival gave skills, abilities, and worldly goods to the church.

Discussion Questions

1. Have you ever been part of a revival where "one disciple awakens another"?

2. How can you welcome the broken into your community and invite them to contribute according to their ability?

Prayer

Lord, I want to sow seeds and be ready for the harvest. I confess that I am not up to the task, and that my narrow and selfish vision often blinds me to the needs of others. As I draw near to you, Father, change my heart. I want to be your vessel and bring other lost sheep into the care of the Great Shepherd.

Amen

Day 30
Jesus is Coming: Repent and Believe
(Hans Nadler)

But about that day or hour no one knows, not even the angels in heaven, nor the Son, but only the Father. As it was in the days of Noah, so it will be at the coming of the Son of Man. For in the days before the flood, people were eating and drinking, marrying and giving in marriage, up to the day Noah entered the ark; and they knew nothing about what would happen until the flood came and took them all away. That is how it will be at the coming of the Son of Man. Two men will be in the field; one will be taken and the other left. Two women will be grinding with a hand mill; one will be taken and the other left. —Matthew 24:36-41

Hans Nadler was an early Anabaptist evangelist who began his ministry immediately after his conversion in 1527 and continued it until his capture and execution two years later. During his interrogation by both government and religious authorities, Hans was asked repeatedly about the timing of the second coming of Christ. Hans would only say that Jesus "will come to judge the living and the dead." His questioners persisted three times with this same question during their interrogation, perhaps trying to catch him declaring a firm date for the end of the world. A belief in the Return of Christ was not unusual at the time, but setting an exact date was considered to be a threat to the state. At each asking, Hans reveals an expectation of Christ's coming that was not tied to any known time or date.

> Who set the day, the hour, or the year, I do not know. No one but the Father knows the day and the hour. But the time is not far away.

For Nadler, the timing of Christ's return was not of primary importance. More important was the fact that Christ was coming *soon*. He exhorted his captors to repent, believe, and adopt a godly lifestyle that would please the Lord when he came back to establish his kingdom.

> I do not know whether the spears are ready, whether he will come in twenty-three hundred or in two hundred or in a thousand years. But the Scripture says: You are all to repent, forsake sin, and turn to God. All that is evil will be destroyed, but the devout and the godly he will take into his kingdom. 'Therefore,' says Christ,

'Struggle to enter by the straight gate' [Matthew 7:13].[37]

Hans believed that Christ would come again, and this conviction provided an urgency to his evangelism. But he would not be drawn into vain discussions about the day and the hour of Christ's return.

Discussion Questions

1. What are the dangers of setting the date for Christ's return?

2. Is a belief in Jesus' Second Coming a good motivation for evangelism? Is it essential for godly living?

---

[37] Hans Nadler, "Declaration of the Needle Merchant Hans at Erlangen and the Refutation of the Articles of the Needle Merchant Hans (1529)," in *Sources of South German/Austrian Anabaptism*, ed. Walter Klaassen et al., *Classics of the Radical Reformation* (Kitchener, ON: Pandora Press; co-published with Herald Press, 2001), 147.

Prayer

Father, I confess that I often live my life without a sense of your intervention in human affairs. My perspective can easily be limited to my immediate needs and aspirations. I need your help to live a holy and productive life in light of eternity, always conscious that you have the whole of human history in your hands, and that you may act quickly to make all things right.

Amen

Postscript
Following Christ in Humility

Eighty years ago, on December 28th 1943, Harold S. Bender gave the presidential address to the American Society for Church History in New York entitled "The Anabaptist Vision." He shared this vision at a dark moment in human history, six months before the Allied invasion of Normandy and nineteen months before atomic bombs were dropped on Japan. As the world struggled in the throes of political despotism, holocaust, economic uncertainty, and countless military and civilian deaths, Bender defined his three-fold vision of sixteenth-century Anabaptism. Bender's essay identifies many of the same themes explored in this book.

First, Bender's Anabaptist vision was fundamentally an orientation of the Christian life towards discipleship – that is, following the teachings and example of Christ in everyday life. Bender showed how the Anabaptists held that the inward transformation of faith should have an outward expression. In short, the focus of Anabaptist Christianity was not faith but following.[38] Next, Bender identified voluntary church membership and a commitment to holy living in community. Adult baptism was the first step in this journey. Living according to the ideals of the New Testament produced a church that practiced economic sharing, separation from the world, and a rejection of worldly values.[39] Finally, Bender highlighted the Anabaptist desire to have love and non-resistance (which was later called pacifism) permeate all human interactions.[40]

The contrast between these three components of the Anabaptist vision and the realities of the Second World War could hardly have been starker: the Anabaptists followed Christ instead of dictatorial governments, practiced voluntary community instead of coercively seeking to order the world, fostered economic sharing instead of mutual destruction, pursued non-resistance instead of military conquest, and cultivated love for their neighbors instead of fear and resentment.

As we have seen in the devotional readings in this book, the Anabaptists did not come with a political agenda that sought to transform the state. They understood that people would not approve of how they sought to follow Christ and were

---

[38] Harold Stauffer Bender, "The Anabaptist Vision," *Church History* 13.1 (1944), 14.
[39] Ibid, 17-20.
[40] Ibid, 21.

prepared to die for their faith. They did not come with a strategic plan for a church or denominational entity in order to expand its programs or gain social recognition with earthly definitions of success. Quite simply, they made an appeal to follow the life and teachings of Christ.

There can be no question that the Anabaptists sometimes struggled to pair their earthly disobedience to princess and bishops with the heavenly obedience that they owed to Christ. They resisted the authority of governments to tell them what they should believe and how they should behave, and instead they emphasized the value of the human conscience grounded on the Word of God. They rejected the threats, coercion, and violence of the established churches, and instead they formed Christian communities bound by mutual concern and committed fellowship. The Anabaptists engaged their world in evangelism and mission and built their churches around what they understood as the pattern provided in the New Testament. While membership was voluntary, it came with high expectations of godly conduct. In order to maintain the purity of their fellowship, they accepted separation (or the 'ban') for those who would not live up to those standards.

Such a radical agenda was bound to be messy. As you engaged devotionally or critically with their words (and with mine) in the meditations above, you may have disagreed with the Anabaptist authors, their approach, or their conclusions. During my own devotional exploration of sixteenth-century Anabaptist writers, I found myself personally challenged by their spirituality and convictions, especially when I saw the world differently than they did or I brought a different set of convictions to bear on the biblical text. And yet I was consistently inspired by their devotion to follow Jesus.

How can we engage with their example of radical obedience today? I believe that at least some of the sixteenth-century Anabaptists may have already provided an answer: as we seek to live according to the teachings and ways of Christ, *radical obedience must be paired with radical humility.* In one example, Pilgram Marpeck reminds a group of Anabaptist congregations that it was because of the devil's pride that he and the other fallen angels were thrown into the abyss. Instead,

This intention of God was proclaimed in the midst of heaven by an angel and is eternally so proclaimed, that all creatures of God should, like the Son of the Father, submit freely and without compulsion to such service and lowliness.[41]

---

[41] Pilgram Marpeck, "The Servants and Service of the Church (1532)," in *The Writings of Pilgram Marpeck*, ed. William Klassen and Walter Klaassen, *Classics of the Radical Reformation* (Kitchener, Ont. ; Scottdale, Pa.: Herald Press, 1978), 551.

For the Anabaptist vision to be lived on earth, the requirement of sacrificial service and humility must be absolute – most especially for Christian leaders. Whenever any leader or institution acts to preserve power over others, even in the interests of self-preservation, or when an ethic of sacrificial service is applied to followers but it is not expected of leaders, these are strong indicators that those leaders and institutions may no longer be walking in the ways of the Master (Matthew 20:24-28). Worse than that, such a leader or institution, as it uses worldly power for its own purposes, may be following in the footsteps of the accuser of our souls rather than those of Christ, as Marpeck suggested. Against this danger, we must prayerfully guard our own hearts.

The piety and discipline of the Anabaptists was tempered by humility in a second way. Their practice of humility was eschatological in nature, extending beyond the short horizon of finite human relationships into eternity. Since Christ was the ultimate judge of the human conscience and the measure of the Anabaptist community, it meant that they attempted to separate in peace when they disagreed. Their eschatological humility enabled them to hold firmly to their convictions while extending grace to those with whom they disagreed. For these Christians, confusing or competing voices were not a reason to stand still, but rather created a new urgency to be disciples of Christ.

In the closing words of his essay on the Anabaptist vision, Bender identifies this same eschatological tension at work. He writes,

> The Anabaptist vision was not a detailed blueprint for the reconstruction of human society, but the Brethren did believe that Jesus intended that the Kingdom of God should be set in the midst of earth, here and now, and this they proposed to do forthwith. We shall not believe, they said, that the Sermon on the Mount or any other vision that He had is only a heavenly vision meant but to keep His followers in tension until the last great day, but we shall practice what He taught, believing that where He walked we can by His grace follow in His steps.[42]

For the Anabaptists who sought to follow in the footsteps of Christ amidst the violence, brokenness, poverty, and immorality of the Second World War, this was no small task, just as it was for the sixteenth-century founders of the tradition. Today, we can join them with the same straightforward confidence that God can and will guide the broken, the poor, and the forgotten to become Jesus'

---

[42] Bender, "The Anabaptist Vision," 24.

disciples, without violence and without coercion, when they put their faith in Him. I urge you to walk on that same journey, and to marry conviction with humility and peaceableness as you follow in the footsteps of Christ.

Bibliography

Note: The Classics of the Radical Reformation series is now published by Plough Publishing, available at: https://www.plough.com/en/books/classics-of-the-radical-reformation

The Schleitheim Confession (1527). Edited by John Howard Yoder. Scottdale, Pa.: Herald Press, 1977.

Bender, Harold Stauffer. "The Anabaptist Vision." *Church History* 13, no. 1 (1944): 3-24.

Braght, Thieleman J. van. *The Bloody Theatre or Martyr's Mirror of the Defenceless Christians Who Baptized Only Upon Confession of Faith, and Who Suffered and Died for the Testimony of Jesus, Their Savior, from the Time of Christ to the Year A.D. 1600*. 28 ed. Scottsdale, Pa.: Herald Press, 2007.

Denck, Hans. "Whether God Is the Cause of Evil (1526)." In *Spiritual and Anabaptist Writers*. Edited by George Huntston Williams, Angel M. Mergal, and Juan de Valdés.vol. 25. Philadelphia: Westminster Press, 1957.

Glock, Paul. "First Defense (1563)." In *Sources of South German/Austrian Anabaptism*. Edited by Walter Klaassen, Werner O. Packull, C. Arnold Snyder, and Frank Friesen. Classics of the Radical

Reformation. Vol. 10. Kitchener, ON: Pandora Press; co-published with Herald Press, 2001.

Glock, Paul. "Letter to His Wife Else (1563)." In *Sources of South German/Austrian Anabaptism*. Edited by Walter Klaassen, Werner O. Packull, C. Arnold Snyder, and Frank Friesen. Classics of the Radical Reformation. vol. 10. Kitchener, ON: Pandora Press; co-published with Herald Press, 2001.

Hubmaier, Balthasar. "A Brief 'Our Father' (1526)." In *Balthasar Hubmaier, Theologian of Anabaptism*. Edited by H. Wayne Pipkin and John Howard Yoder. Classics of the Radical Reformation. Vol. 5. Scottdale, Pa.; Kitchener, ON: Herald Press, 1989.

Hubmaier, Balthasar. "On Heretics and Those Who Burn Them (1524)." In *Balthasar Hubmaier, Theologian of Anabaptism*. Edited by H. Wayne Pipkin and John Howard Yoder. Classics of the Radical Reformation. Vol. 5. Scottdale, Pa.; Kitchener, ON: Herald Press, 1989.

Hubmaier, Balthasar. "On the Christian Baptism of Believers (1525)." In *Balthasar Hubmaier, Theologian of Anabaptism*. Edited by H. Wayne Pipkin and John Howard Yoder. Classics of the Radical Reformation. Vol. 5. Scottdale, Pa.; Kitchener, ON: Herald Press, 1989.

Hubmaier, Balthasar. "On the Sword (1525)." In *Balthasar Hubmaier, Theologian of Anabaptism*. Edited by H. Wayne Pipkin and John Howard Yoder. Classics of the Radical Reformation. Vol. 5. Scottdale, Pa.; Kitchener, ON: Herald Press, 1989.

Hutter, Jakob. "Letter 5 (1535)." In *Brotherly Faithfulness: Epistles from a Time of Persecution*. Anabaptist Texts in Translation. Rifton, N.Y.: Plough Pub. House, 2006.

Hutter, Jakob. "Letter 7 (1535)." In *Brotherly Faithfulness: Epistles from a Time of Persecution*. Anabaptist Texts in Translation. Rifton, N.Y.: Plough Pub. House, 2006.

Hutterian Brethren. *The Chronicle of the Hutterian Brethren*. Vol. 1. 2 vols. Rifton, N.Y.; Ste. Agathe, Man.: Plough Publishing House, 1987.

Marpeck, Pilgram. "An Epistle Concerning the Heritage and Service of Sin (1545)." In *The Writings of Pilgram Marpeck*. Edited by William Klassen and Walter Klaassen. Classics of the Radical Reformation. Vol. 2. Kitchener, ON; Scottdale, Pa.: Herald Press, 1978.

Nadler, Hans. "Declaration of the Needle Merchant Hans at Erlangen and the Refutation of the Articles of the Needle Merchant Hans (1529)." In *Sources of South German/Austrian Anabaptism*. Edited by Walter Klaassen, Werner O. Packull, C. Arnold

Snyder, and Frank Friesen. Classics of the Radical Reformation. Vol. 10. Kitchener, ON: Pandora Press; co-published with Herald Press, 2001.

Sattler, Michael. "Parting with the Strasbourg Reformers (1526)." In *The Legacy of Michael Sattler*. Edited by John Howard Yoder. Classics of the Radical Reformation. Vol. 1. Scottdale, Pa.: Herald Press, 1973.

Schlaffer, Hans. "Instruction on Beginning a True Christian Life (1527)." In *Early Anabaptist Spirituality: Selected Writings*. Edited by Daniel Liechty. New York: Paulist Press, 1994.

Schlaffer, Hans. "Two Prayers (1527)." In *Early Anabaptist Spirituality: Selected Writings*. Edited by Daniel Liechty. New York: Paulist Press, 1994.

Schmidt, Hans. "Hans Schmidt's Experiences in Württemberg (1590)." In *Sources of South German/Austrian Anabaptism*. Edited by Walter Klaassen, Werner O. Packull, C. Arnold Snyder, and Frank Friesen. Classics of the Radical Reformation. Vol. 10. Kitchener, ON: Pandora Press; co-published with Herald Press, 2001.

Simons, Menno. "Christian Baptism (1539)." In *The Complete Writings of Menno Simons, C. 1496-1561*. Edited by J. C. Wenger and Harold Stauffer Bender. Scottdale, Pa.; Kitchener, ON: Herald Press, 1986.

Simons, Menno. "Encouragement to Christian Believers (1556)." In *The Complete Writings of Menno Simons, C. 1496-1561*. Edited by J. C. Wenger and Harold Stauffer Bender. Scottdale, Pa.; Kitchener, ON: Herald Press, 1986.

Simons, Menno. "Foundation of Christian Doctrine (1539)." In *The Complete Writings of Menno Simons, C. 1496-1561*. Edited by J. C. Wenger and Harold Stauffer Bender. Scottdale, Pa.; Kitchener, ON: Herald Press, 1986.

Simons, Menno. "A Meditation on the Twenty-Fifth Psalm (1537)." In *Early Anabaptist Spirituality: Selected Writings*. Edited by Daniel Liechty. New York: Paulist Press, 1994.

Simons, Menno. "Reply to False Accusations (1552)." In *The Complete Writings of Menno Simons, C. 1496-1561*. Edited by J. C. Wenger and Harold Stauffer Bender. Scottdale, Pa.; Kitchener, ON: Herald Press, 1986.

Spitelmaier, Ambrosius. "Questions and Answers of Ambrosius Spitelmaier (1527)." In *Sources of South German/Austrian Anabaptism*. Edited by Walter Klaassen, Werner O. Packull, C. Arnold Snyder, and Frank Friesen. Classics of the Radical Reformation. Vol. 10. Kitchener, ON: Pandora Press; co-published with Herald Press, 2001.

About the Author

Colin Godwin serves as the President of Carey Theological College in Vancouver, Canada. He was born in Belgium and educated at the University of Guelph, the University of St. Michael's College, McMaster University, and the University of Wales. He began his ministry as a youth pastor and served as a Baptist missionary in Belgium, Rwanda, and Kenya alongside the love of his life, Karen, and their four children. Colin is the author of an exploration of sixteenth-century Anabaptist missiology, *Baptizing, Gathering and Sending: the significance of Anabaptist approaches to mission in the sixteenth-century context* (Pandora Press, 2012), and articles on Baptist and Anabaptist history, church planting, and missiology.

Pandora Press is an independent publisher focusing on scholarly and popular titles in Anabaptist Mennonite Studies and beyond.

For a catalogue of recent publications, details for submitting manuscripts, and contact information please see our website: www.pandorapress.com

www.ingramcontent.com/pod-product-compliance
Lightning Source LLC
Chambersburg PA
CBHW031134090426
42738CB00008B/1087